Vets Can Fix It

Written by
Cath Jones

The pets are in the waiting room at the vets.

The pets are unwell or hurt.

They are waiting for a vet to see them.

Vets see parrots, rats and rabbits too.

The vet checks to see if the pet is in pain.

This dog has a pain in her tail and a nail in her foot.

The dog wails in pain.
It hurts!

The vet can fix it ...
and now the dog
licks the vet!

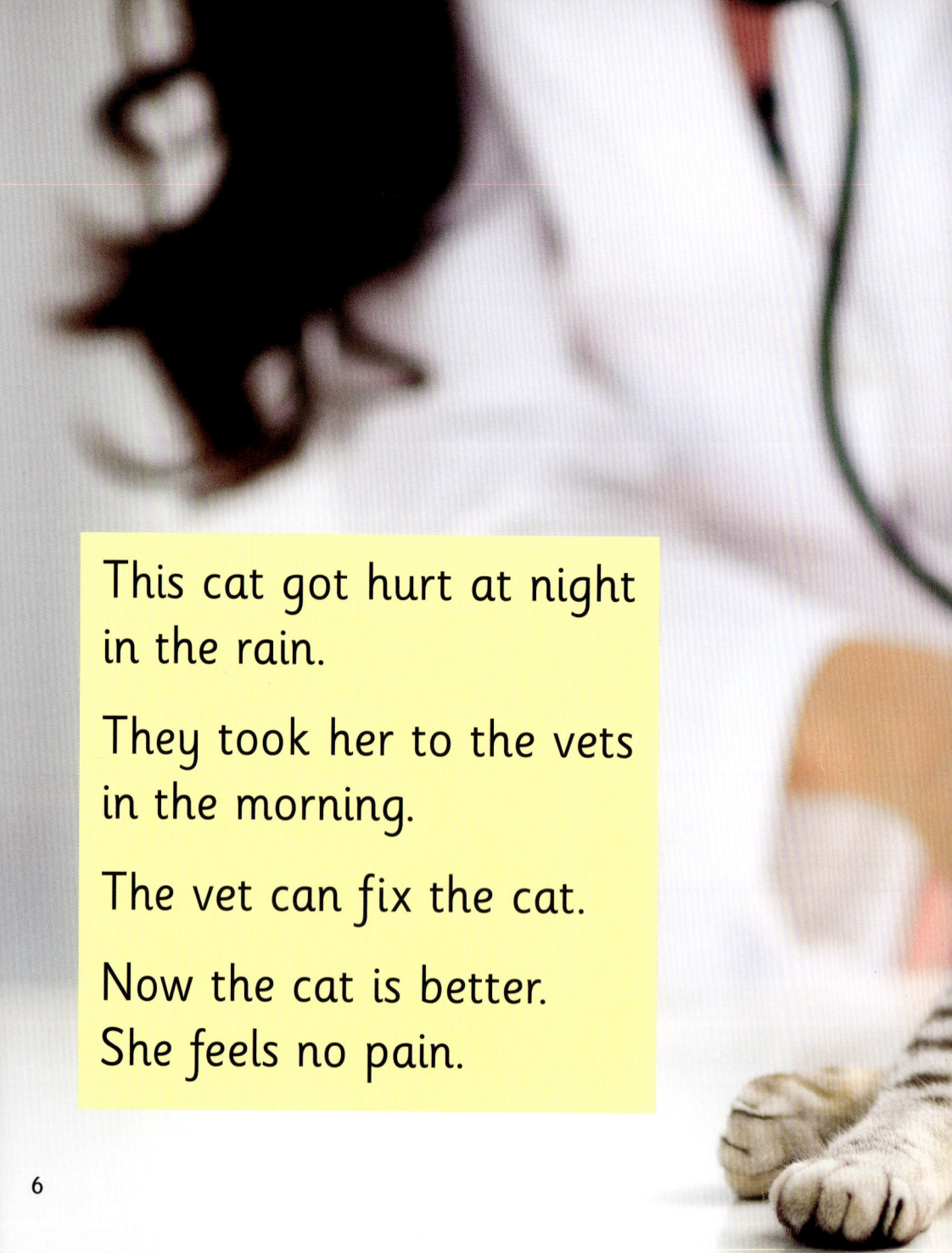

This cat got hurt at night in the rain.

They took her to the vets in the morning.

The vet can fix the cat.

Now the cat is better. She feels no pain.

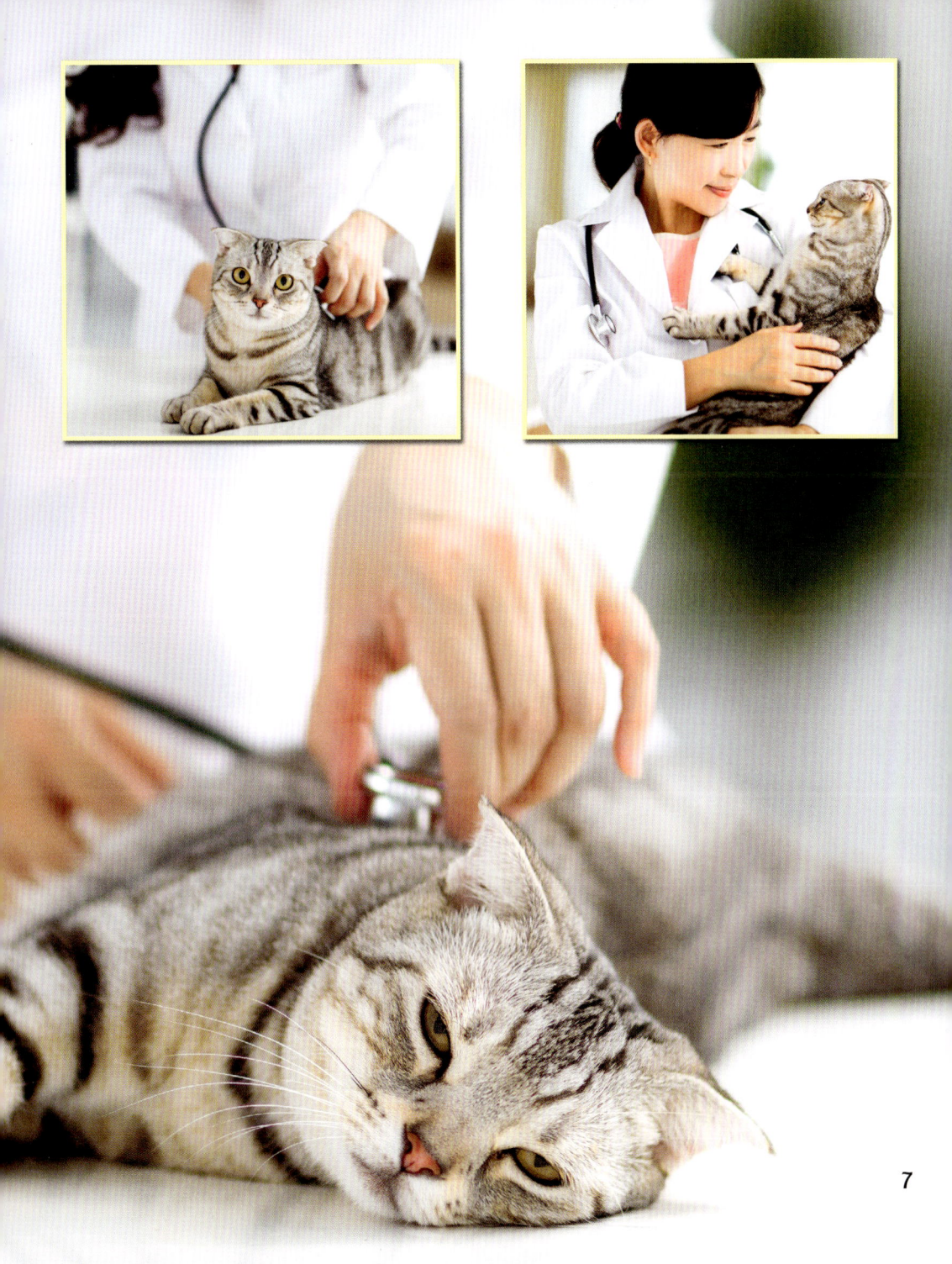

This vet needs to pop down to the farm in her car.

She visits the farm in the rain and the hail and the fog.

She will get wet at the farm!

The vet checks the goats.
Are they in pain?

The vet looks at the goat's hoof.
The hoof is good.

But wait! Are the goat's teeth good?
The vet checks the goat's teeth.

This goat is good.
He is fit and has no pain.

11

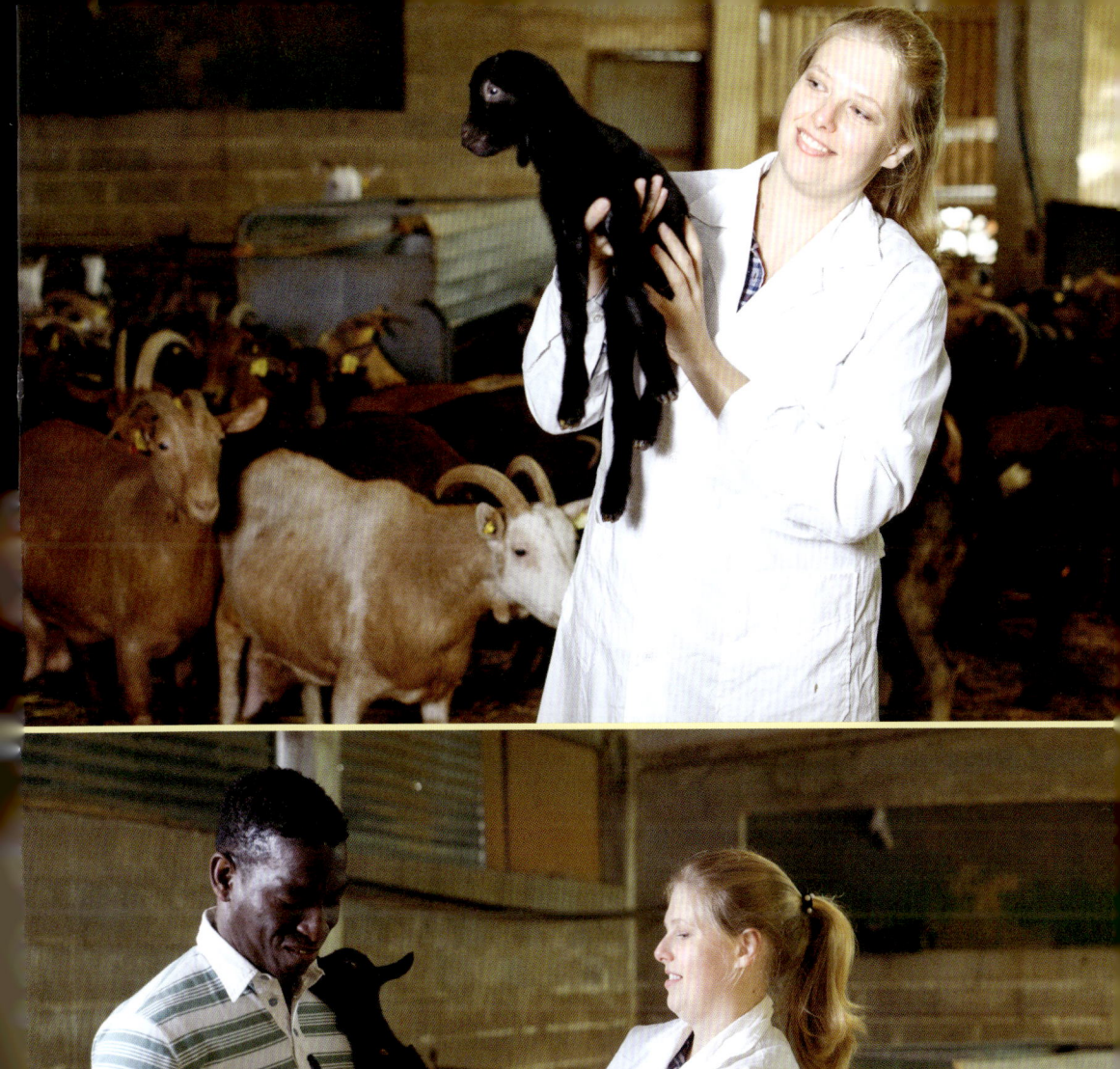

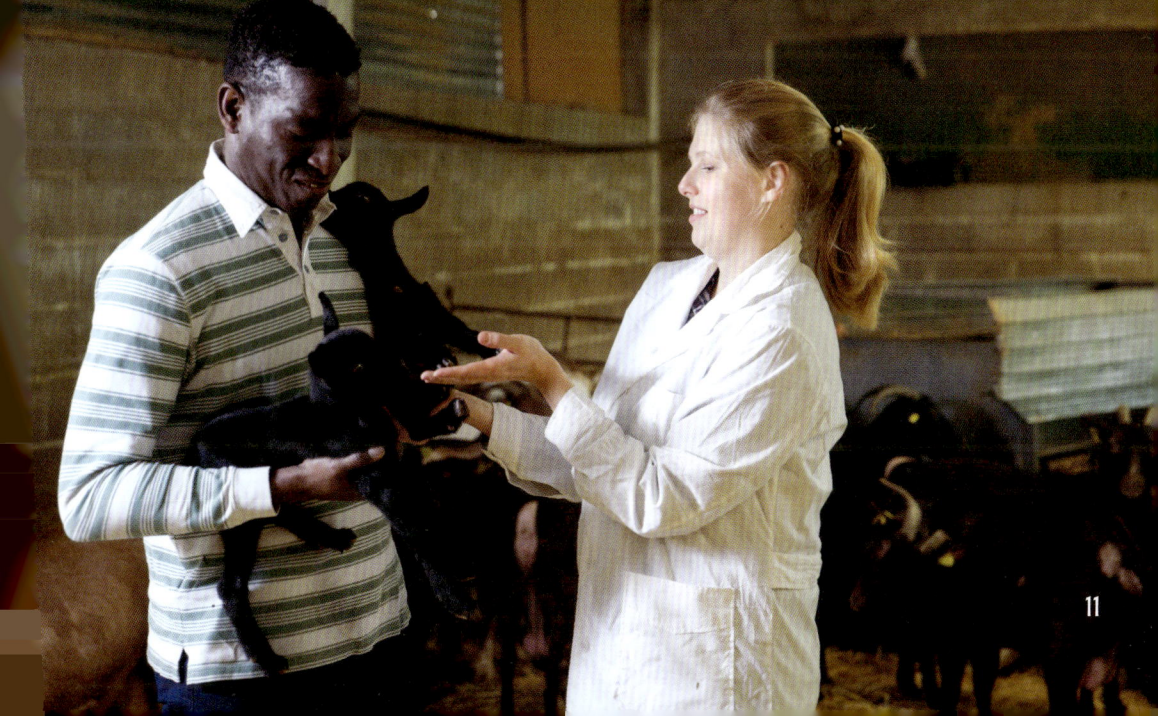

Now the farmer has paid the vet's big bill.

The vet can go back to town.

Top job, vets!